ZOO BABIES

Wilbur and Orville the Otter Twins

Story by **Georgeanne Irvine**

Photographs by **Ron Garrison**

of the **Zoological Society of San Diego**

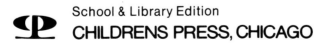

School & Library Edition

CHILDRENS PRESS, CHICAGO

Library of Congress Cataloging in Publication Data

Irvine, Georgeanne.
  Wilbur and Orville, the otter twins.

  (Zoo babies)
  Includes index.
  Summary: Text and pictures show two baby
otters, residents of a zoo, during their first
three months of life.
    1. Otters—Juvenile literature.
2. Animals, Infancy of—Juvenile literature.
3. Zoo animals—Juvenile literature.
[1. Otters. 2. Animals—Infancy. 3. Zoo
animals] I. Garrison, Ron, ill. II. Title.
III. Series.
QL737.C25I78   1982   599.74'447   82-9451
ISBN 0-516-09305-3   AACR2

ZOO BABIES

Wilbur and Orville the Otter Twins

The first time an animal mother has babies, she isn't always ready to take care of them. That's exactly what happened to our mother—and to us, Wilbur and Orville, the otters at the Zoo.

Mother otters, with a little help from father otters, usually build a nest of leaves, sticks, and mud before their otter pups are born.

We surprised our parents because we were born before they had built a nest!

Conny and Kristi, the otter keepers at the Zoo, realized our mother wasn't ready to raise a family of otters. They decided it would be safer to have substitute human mothers care for us in the animal nursery.

When we went to live in the nursery, we looked like fuzzy little puppies. We were helpless. We didn't have any teeth, and our eyes weren't open yet.

The nursery attendants—our human mothers—had to stay with us day and night. After all, we were very hungry. We had to be fed milk formula every two hours!

We were so tiny, the attendants used to feed us with an eyedropper! It didn't take much formula to fill us. We grew quickly. Our nursery mothers were soon feeding us with a doll bottle instead of an eyedropper.

Our eyes finally opened when we were six weeks old. At last, we could see what was going on around us! We noticed that our light gray fur was slowly changing to a dark chocolate brown.

By the time we were nine weeks old, we still looked like puppies—furry brown puppies.

Whenever we took our naps, we had to be right next to each other or else we would make loud chirping noises and squeaks.

One day, Conny and Kristi announced it was time for us to learn how to swim. Conny and Kristi said all otters are good swimmers because they usually live near a river, a stream, or a sea. Since we were otters, we had to learn to swim, too. Once we learned to swim, we would live in the big otter exhibit. There we could swim in the pond, slip down the slide, and explore our new home.

How were we going to learn to swim? An otter mother teaches her pups how to swim when they're a few months old. She pushes her pups into the water, and soon they are swimming right behind her. Sometimes, otter pups even ride on their mother's back.

We weren't being raised by our mother. Who was going to teach us to swim?

Our problem was soon solved. Our nursery mothers were going to be our swimming teachers.

Conny and Kristi took us to the big otter enclosure. Each of them held one of us and waded into the water. They tossed us into the water, and we swam back to them. Swimming was easy! It seemed as if we had always known how to swim.

Conny and Kristi gave us lessons every day for several weeks. Each day after our lessons, they dried us with a towel and let us sit in their laps in the sun for awhile.

When we were three months old, we didn't need our nursery mothers to help us swim anymore. We stopped drinking milk and began eating fish, meat, and eggs.

It was time for us to live in the big otter enclosure where we could swim and slide and play and explore—just like the other otters.

Facts About Otters

Where found: Otters live everywhere in the world except Australia. There are several kinds, including those that live in freshwater lakes and rivers and those that live in the Pacific Ocean (sea otters).

Family: Otters are members of the weasel family.

Baby otters: The babies, called pups, are born blind. Their eyes open after about six weeks. They learn to swim when they are two or three months old.

Adult otters: Most types are from three to four feet long and weigh about ten to twenty pounds. The giant otter, found only in South America, can grow to be as long as seven feet.

Food: Otters are meat eaters. They catch all kinds of fish, shellfish, frogs, and even snakes and insects.

Paws: Otters are able to use their clawed paws to hold things, such as the food they eat.

Fur: The fur of otters can be chocolate brown to gray or any shade in between. It looks very dark—almost black—when wet. Like other swimming animals, otters have a double coat of fur. The undercoat is short, very thick, and keeps the otter dry when swimming. The outercoat, called guard hair, is long and protects the undercoat.

Swimming: Otters' bodies are perfect for swimming. They are long, sleek animals, with small heads, long necks, and long pointed tails. Their ears and noses close when swimming, to keep water out. They have webbing between their toes to help them to swim.

Play: Otters are among the most playful animals on earth. They run around in otter games of chase, sometimes jumping on each other and wrestling. They like to slide down riverbanks into the water, just as people slide down man-made slides into swimming pools. They "talk" to each other with all sorts of noises—chirps, squeaks, squeals, growls, and even a kind of high-pitched laughter.

INDEX